The Let's Talk Library™

Let's Talk About When Your Pet Dies

Marianne Johnston

The Rosen Publishing Group's
PowerKids Press™
New York

Published in 1997 by The Rosen Publishing Group, Inc.
29 East 21st Street, New York, NY 10010

First Edition

Book design: Erin McKenna

Photo credits: Cover photo by Carrie Ann Grippo; p. 7 © Dusty Willison/International Stock; p. 12 © Caroline Wood/International Stock; all other photos by Carrie Ann Grippo.

Johnston, Marianne.
    Let's talk about when your pet dies / Marianne Johnston.
        p.   cm. — (The Let's talk library)
    Includes index.
    Summary: Describes the feelings that you might have when your pet dies and discusses how to cope with these feelings.
    ISBN 0-8239-5039-5
    1. Pet owners—Psychology—Juvenile literature. 2. Pets—Death—Psychological aspects—Juvenile literature. 3. Bereavement—Psychological aspects—Juvenile literature. 4. Children and animals—Juvenile literature. 5. Children and death—Juvenile literature. [1. Pets—Death. 2. Death. 3. Grief.] I. Title. II. Series.
SF411.47.J64 1996
155.9'37—dc20   96-32582
                                                            CIP
                                                            AC

Manufactured in the United States of America

Table of Contents

What Is a Pet?

A pet is a lot more than just a cute animal who lives in your house. Pets can become part of your family. A pet can cheer you up when you're unhappy, or keep you company when you're lonely or bored. Your pet is an important part of your life. When that part of your life is gone, it can be painful and sad. It may feel like a member of your family has died.

Pets become part of your family. ▶

How Pets Die

Sometimes pets die in **accidents** (AK-sih-dents), like Shawna's dog, Chief, did. Other times pets are so sick or in so much pain that they won't ever get better. They have to be "put to sleep." This means that the **veterinarian** (vet-ur-in-AYR-ee-en), or animal doctor, will give your pet a shot that helps her die without any pain at all. This may seem like a terrible thing to do. But your pet is hurting. She will never stop hurting. It is nicer to your pet to put her to sleep than to keep her alive and hurting all the time.

◀ Sometimes sick or hurting pets have to be put to sleep by the veterinarian.

When You Lose a Pet

When your pet dies, you lose more than a **playmate** (PLAY-mayt). You lose a part of yourself and a big part of your life. You may have many feelings when your pet dies. You may be angry and upset. Or you may feel sad and lonely. You may not feel anything at all for a while. It is normal to have any or all of these feelings. Losing a pet is hard.

You may feel sad and upset when your pet dies. It is normal to feel this way. ▶

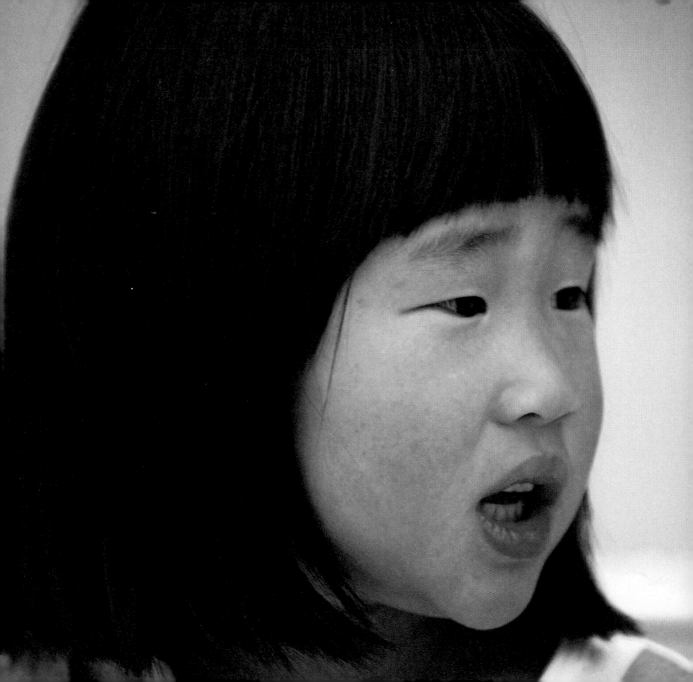

It's Okay to Cry

You will probably feel very sad when your pet dies. You may even want to cry. It's okay to cry. Crying is your body's way of getting rid of sadness. Some people don't like to cry in front of others. They are afraid of what other people will think. But crying is the best way to let others know you are sad. If others know you are sad, they can help you feel better.

◀ Don't be afraid to cry if you feel like it.

Blaming Someone

You may be angry when your pet dies. You may want to **blame** (BLAYM) someone. If your pet was put to sleep, you may blame the veterinarian or your parents. If your pet was hit by a car, you may blame the driver of the car. If you find yourself doing this, remember two things. First, blaming people won't bring your pet back. Second, it's okay to feel angry, but it's not okay to take it out on other people. Talk to someone, such as a parent or teacher, about your feelings. He or she can help you find a better way to get rid of your anger.

You may want to take your angry feelings out on your ▶ family members. But remember that they're sad, too.

Remembering Your Pet

At first you might try to forget about your pet. Thinking about him can be sad and painful. Keeping your sadness inside won't make it go away. But talking about your pet will help. Talking about your pet may be hard at first. But soon you will be thinking more about the good times you had with him and less about his death. You might even ask your mom or dad to put a picture of your pet on the refrigerator.

◄ Trying to forget about your pet won't make the pain or sadness go away.

Funny Stories

Once you begin to talk about your pet, you will start to feel better. You and your family can share funny stories about your pet. You can talk about some of the things you liked best about her. You can talk about her death, too. Ask your parents about anything you don't understand. You may be **confused** (kon-FYOOZD) about how or why your pet died. Your parents may have some or all of the answers. Chances are they loved your pet as much as you did.

Talking about the good times with your pet can help make you and your family feel better. ▶

The Next Pet

You and your family may **decide** (dee-SIDE) to get a new pet. The new pet won't take the place of the pet that died. But it will have its own place in your heart and in your family. You may be scared that this pet will die, too. It is normal to feel this way. But when you think about the good parts of having a pet, you'll see that having a pet is worth the **risk** (RISK) of losing a pet.

◀ Getting a new pet doesn't mean that you've forgotten your other pet. It just means that you have a new pet to love.

Lisa and Her Cat

Lisa cried for days when her cat died. She missed Tommy so much that she thought the pain would never go away. At first she didn't even want to think about him. But then Lisa talked with her parents about Tommy. She explained how Tommy would climb into her bed in the mornings. He would nudge his nose against Lisa's nose to wake her up. Talking about the good times with Tommy made Lisa feel much better.

Glossary

accident (AK-sih-dent) Something harmful or unlucky that happens when you are not expecting it.

blame (BLAYM) To hold someone responsible for something bad or wrong.

confuse (kon-FYOOZ) To mix up.

decide (dee-SIDE) To make up your mind.

playmate (PLAY-mayt) Friend.

risk (RISK) Chance of harm or loss.

veterinarian (vet-ur-in-AYR-ee-en) Animal doctor.

Index